FAREWELL
THE LAST SERMON OF OUR BELOVED

FAREWELL – THE LAST SERMON OF OUR BELOVED ﷺ

First published in Malaysia by
Tertib Publishing
23-2 Jalan PJS 5/30
Petaling Jaya Commercial City (PJCC)
46150 Petaling Jaya, Selangor
Malaysia

Tel: +603 7772 3156

First Edition: February 2020

ISBN: 978-967-2420-03-3

Cover design: Ahmad Zahin Zulkipli
Transcription: Hanis Tahir
Typesetting & Layout: Ainul Syuhada
Printed by: Firdaus Press Sdn. Bhd.

Contents

PREFACE

All praises due to Allah *subhanahu wa ta'ala* (S.W.T) who knows what we reveal. The One who knows what we conceal and even knows what the animals feel. We thank Him, we praise Him and on Him we have reliance. It is to Him we only turn to for our true guidance and we ask Him to send His peace, blessings and mercy on the best of human beings and prophets, Muhammad *sallahualaihi wa salam* (S.A.W). On whom we praise until the very end of our days and we ask Him to send us our Prophet S.A.W's peace, guidance, mercy, to never lead us astray and for him to save us on Judgment Day. Ameen.

FOREWORD

The Farewell Sermon by Prophet Muhammad *Sallahualaihi Wa Salam* (S.A.W - Peace be upon him) was conveyed more than 1400 years ago. It is a piece of history that may have been heard since the childhood times but miraculously remain to be leaving profound reminders to every heart and soul as the story is visited.

In the process of transcribing this magnificent event, a journey of self-recall to the very first time reading and listening to the story of the farewell sermon by Prophet Muhammad S.A.W was experienced, but this time around, it was more in depth of meaning and understanding from it. The reminders that were touching to the heart when the story was first heard still remain to be impactful even after more than ten times of hearing it.

Glory be to Allah, for that is Islam. A religion that is from Allah *As-Samad*, The Eternal. The religion of guidance that came from the time of our Father, Prophet Adam *Alaihi Salam* and still remain relevant to this day; ageless and everlasting. Therefore, just as other reminders in Islam effortlessly remain pertinent, this book strives to carve significant impacts during the first read and hope to remain the same when it is read again in the future.

Farewell: The Last Sermon of Our Beloved is a light reading for those who are just beginning to indulge themselves in reading books of faith, but still remain impactful for the avid readers as well. Delivered by Shaykh Hasib Noor, whose life was filled with seeking knowledge from various parts of the world such as Madinah and the United States; with over 10 years of experience working in national and international organisation. He has held various positions as a board member of organisation, *masajid* and as a *khatib*.

The Prophet Muhammad S.A.W said "Convey from me, even if it is one verse.." (Sahih Bukhari)

Tertib Publishing | tertib.press

Chapter 1

The Yearning of Prophet Muhammad S.A.W's Love

Our Prophet Muhammad *alaihi salatu wa salam*, our *habib* before he left this world, he gave a powerful admonition. He said "If one of you is afflicted with a calamity, then let him remember his calamity by me (Prophet S.A.W's death); for indeed, it is the greatest of calamities" (Ibn Majah). However, before our beloved Prophet *alaihi salatu wa salam* left this world, he reminded us that even in his passing, he gave us the best of guidance of what to do after his passing. He told us how to carry on the legacy of *Rasulullah* S.A.W. That even knowing that we would lose *Rasulullah* S.A.W, he gave us the best of guidance on how to deal with his loss.

Imagine the most beloved person to us, whether it was our grandmother, mother, father or somebody that means a lot to us; just the thought and pain of knowing that we would depart from them one day from this world is so painful. Some of us don't even want to think about it. Imagine, that person that we love, before they leave this world, they stop us and give some advices. How meaningful would those advices be? This is the example of our Prophet S.A.W, who is the most beloved to all of the Muslims in this world, no matter where they are. Imagine the *sahabahs* who saw him every single day, saw his beautiful smile and his presence was a comfort for them. Not only as a comfort in their lives of difficulty and hardship, but the presence of S.A.W made their hearts seek comfort and solace.

Many of us may have looked at a picture of Madinah; many of us who have been there, we just look at the picture and we find comfort, solace and peace. This is because Madinah is the city of comfort and peace. The city where if we go, we feel like this is our home. We feel like this is how it should be. Many people travelled all over the world such as businessmen, been in the best hotels, first class airlines, and everywhere in this world. They have mentioned that they have never been somewhere that as soon as they step on the earth, they feel they're at home and in the city of the Prophet S.A.W. Why? Because of the presence of *Rasulullah* S.A.W.

The Prophet Muhammad S.A.W's presence brought peace to the *sahabahs*. Imagine simply our thoughts now on him, brings us peace. Saying *allahumma salli ala sayyidina* Muhammad, brings us peace. Imagine what it was like for the *sahabahs* to know one day they would depart from him. How difficult and painful was it from them? Many of us depart from Madinah, we know how painful and difficult that is. And we ask Allah to please bring us back there or we say "Oh Allah, join me with the *Rasulullah* S.A.W". Imagine ourselves being the *sahabahs* and hearing from the Prophet S.A.W for the very last time during his final sermon.

Chapter 2

Love of the Ansar
for Prophet S.A.W

Prophet Muhammad S.A.W gave his last *khutbah* to the people of Madinah, publicly. Many of us know the farewell sermon and we know the *khutbah* was called *khutbatul wada'*. A lot of us may have not studied in depth that the Prophet S.A.W had this final sermon in the last two days before he passed away. He gathered the people in Madinah and our tradition preserve this through *khutbah* of Friday prayer to this day.

Prophet S.A.W said "One day, Abu Bakr and Abbas (the uncle of Prophet S.AW.), during the final weeks before Prophet Muhammad's passing, the final days; passed by one of the gatherings of the Ansar, they saw them sitting in the masjid of Prophet S.A.W weeping and crying." These are the Ansar, the people of Madinah, the people of Prophet S.A.W. Those who welcomed our Prophet *alaihi salatu wa salam.*

Abu Bakr & Abbas then asked them "Why are you weeping?" The Ansar replied "We are weeping because we remember the gatherings we had with Prophet S.A.W. And we know that he's going to pass away very soon." So Abu Bakr and Abbas then went to the Prophet S.A.W and told him of that. *Nabi* S.A.W loved the Ansar so much that he did not want to even hear that they would be in pain. This is our Prophet, he loves the believers so much, and he could not bear in his sickness at the time of his passing, to hear that another Muslim is sad.

What did Prophet S.A.W do? While in sickness, while coming in and out of consciousness. While the pain is going through his body *alaihi salatu wa salam*. He was lying in the home of his wife, Aisha *radiallahu anha*; he told his family "Pour over me seven buckets of water from seven different wells in Madinah so that I can go address the people." Our Prophet *alaihi salatu wa salam* was in such pain, that he needed seven buckets of water on him so that he could have some energy to be able to speak.

Being in that pain, can we imagine someone so selfless, he still wanted to assure his community. People who were weeping and crying of his loss, he wanted to go to speak to them. So Prophet S.A.W then came out, being carried by his companions and went to his mimbar while his head is tied with a sheet because his head was having a severe headache. It is reported by Anas ibn Malik who said "He ascended the mimbar which he will never ascend after that day."

Imagine what the companions felt after seeing that. Imagine being in Masjid An-Nabawi and seeing the same mimbar of Prophet S.A.W climbed it. Anas ibn Malik is describing that. The Prophet S.A.W climbed his mimbar and he would never climb it again after that day. He said that the Prophet Muhammad S.A.W stood and glorified, praised and thanked Allah S.W.T.

Prophet Muhammad S.A.W then mentioned Ashab Uhud – The Battle of Uhud; those who sacrificed for Islam on the day of Uhud. He mentioned those like his uncle, Hamzah who passed away. He mentioned those like Saad ibn Rabi' *radiallahu anhu* (R.A); one of the greatest of the Ansar who passed away. He mention Uhud, which he did *istighfar*, asked Allah to forgive them and made dua'a for them.

And then Prophet Muhammad S.A.W said to his companions "Oh Muhajireen, my followers that were with me since the beginning, those who migrated to Madinah and you came from outside the city. You have increased and kept increasing. Many people will come to Islam from the outside and they will migrate to Madinah." It was noted that the number of Ansar have not been able to beat the increment because the Muslims from outside of Madinah kept increasing faster than the people of Ansar.

Prophet Muhammad S.A.W then continued "I advise you and request you to take care of the Ansar; the people of Madinah. They are my near and dear companions; my family." He called the Ansar were those who have a symbionic relationship with him; meaning he can't survive without them. He calls them his family and a family is only those who we confide our deepest secrets to. He told the closest companions to take care of them. Why? Because the Ansar were the ones crying over his loss.

The Ansar were in the masjid, remembering the sittings with the Prophet S.A.W, where Abu bakr and Abbas then passed by and they were the ones who have a heavy heart. Prophet S.A.W loved them because they loved the Prophet S.A.W. He said "They have fulfilled their obligations. Everything that Allah has wanted them to do, they have already done them. And what is left of them, is what Allah S.W.T has in store for them in rewards. So accept from the good that they have and overlook their mistakes". Why our *habib* gave his final *khutbah* with these words? Speaking about the Ansar and what the Ansar did for *Rasulullah* S.A.W? Because he wanted the rest of the ummah to be like the Ansar.

Chapter 3

Genuine Brotherhood of the Ansar

In the first part of the final *khutbah*, Prophet Muhammad S.A.W reminded the ummah of the Ansar. Remember that the Ansar were the ones who welcomed their homes to *Rasulullah* S.A.W. Understand what their level was and this is in a few mentions of the events of the lives of the Ansar. When the Prophet S.A.W arrived, he implemented in Islam something that humanity had never seen before and that is called brotherhood. That brotherhood was an obligation in Islam and if they were from the citizens of Madinah, open their house to the refugees or migrant (Muhajireen). It was an obligation and they did it with love.

Many of the great companions we know like Abu Bakr R.A, he was hosted by an Ansari named Kharija ibn Zaid. Abdurrahman ibn Auf who was a multimillionaire in Makkah, lost all of his wealth as he migrated and what happened? He was welcomed in the home of Saad ibn Rabi'. When Abdurrahman ibn Auf came to the home of Saad Ibn Rabi', he said to Abdurrahman ibn Auf, "I am the richest among all of the Ansar, so I want to divide the property between us." He said something so powerful and with such great faith that we can't understand what he was thinking. Saad said "I have two wives, whichever one you like, I will divorce her and you can marry her." This is out of his love for his brother.

What did Abdurrahman do? Abdurrahman said "May Allah bless your family and your wealth, show me the market place" because he's a businessman. He didn't want to take advantage of Saad, but he was going to take what was necessary and go do business. Allah S.W.T blessed Abdurrahman in business and in his heritage, he had 22 million dollars left after he passed away. He became so rich in Madinah, his home was the guesthouse of the Prophet Muhammad S.A.W. His home was called Darul Diyafa - The home that Prophet Muhammad S.A.W would have his guests. Why? Because of their genuineness.

Why did Prophet Muhammad S.A.W mentioned in his final *khutbah* about the Ansar? He wanted us as the Muslim ummah to be the Ansar. He wants us as an ummah to live the love of the Ansar for *Rasulullah* S.A.W. Imagine the Ansar in the masjid during the *khutbah*, what were they thinking about? Were they thinking what am I going to do? How many days am I going to take off? Am I losing my business? No. They said they were going to miss Prophet S.A.W and they were crying in the masjid. Prophet S.A.W didn't even pass away yet at that time. Imagine the love that they had and the Prophet S.A.W loved them back. Why? Because they were genuine people.

When an Ansar helped someone, it wasn't with the thought of "What are they going to give me back?" Whether it was their friend, neighbor, sister, worker, co-worker, or anyone, they were genuine. What did Allah do? Allah says "If you were genuine in your faith, Allah S.W.T blesses you and He blesses the person that you're going to help." If we're a society that is genuinely helping, Allah will bless us and the people we're trying to help. This is called faith.

Faith is something that we cannot see, we cannot compute and we cannot take a calculator and say "Hey if I give $10, my paycheck will come next month and that will make up for it." That's not what faith is. Faith is this person is in need, "What can I do to fulfill all of your need? Because I know, that Allah is more kind than I am." Allah is *Asy-Syakur*, the name means He rewards us exponentially; more than we could ever give, beyond our wildest imaginations and dream. This is what the Ansar knew. Immediately when faith enters the heart of the Ansar, they helped people knowing that Allah S.W.T is kinder than they are.

Chapter 4

Selflessness of the Ansar

Abu Hurairah R.A mentioned another genuine moment of love and faith that the Ansar had. A man came to the Prophet S.A.W. Prophet S.A.W then sent a messenger to his family to bring something for this man to eat. When the wives of Prophet S.A.W gave him news, they said "We don't have anything to give him". Can we imagine that our Prophet Muhammad S.A.W would spend his life and there were times when there was no food in his home? But our Prophet S.A.W would think of others and say is there any food for them? Sometimes the *sahabahs* would go to Prophet S.A.W's house and they would ask "Ya *Rasulullah*, do you have any food?" and the Prophet S.A.W never complained in his life, so he raised his shirt to his companions showing he had rocks tied onto his stomach out of hunger.

This is our *habib alaihi salatu wa salam*. When Prophet S.AW's wives came and gave him the news "Ya *Rasulullah*, we have nothing in our house, except water". Allah's Messenger S.A.W said "Then who will take this person and entertain him as my guest, because I can't do so". Can we imagine our Prophet was such a kind and selfless person that he did not even want this guest to remain without someone hosting him. This is who the Ansar were. They were the ones who hosted Prophet S.A.W's guests. An Ansari man then stood up and said "I will, ya *Rasulullah*".

The Ansari man took the guest home to his own wife and said to her "Entertain generously the guest of Allah's Messenger S.A.W." So she said "We have nothing to give except for the meals which were prepared to give their own children." He then said "Prepare your meal. Light your lamp and let your children sleep. If they ask for supper, let them play and keep them busy in this play." So she prepared her lamp and made her children sleep. Then she stood up pretending to adjust the lamp, making it darker. Then both of them pretended to eat, while their guest ate the food. In reality, when their guest finished eating, they put the food away and they went to bed hungry.

In the morning, the Ansari went to the messenger S.A.W who said "Tonight, Allah in the heavens, smiled over for what you did today". Because they only did it for Allah. The lesson from the Ansar was it is not what we do in public, it is that every moment, we use is to exercise that Allah is watching us. The Ansar learned that their day to day helping is a *muamalah* with Allah S.W.T. It is a dealing with Allah, our Lord. They didn't think about the public, they dealt with what's in front of them day to day. Regardless if it is a worker on the street. Regardless if it is somebody that comes to us in their need, we would have 30,000 doubts that *shaitaan* brings in our head.

The first and only thing that should come to our mind "How is my dealing with Allah going to be with this?" That's the Ansar. That's *Rasulullah* S.A.W. He didn't even think about "What's in my house?" before he hosted the guest. The Prophet instantly said "I will host you!" then his family came and told him "There's nothing except water ya *Rasulullah*." Did he reject the guest? No, he asked "Who would host my guest?" Allahu akbar. Then what happened? He said "Tonight Allah smiled and wondered over your actions."

Allah then revealed a verse in the Qur'an which praised the Ansar and the Muslims till the Day of Judgement will read this. They are so amazing that Allah revealed a chapter and verses about them. Allah S.W.T said "And [also for] those who were settled in al-Madinah and [adopted] the faith before them.

They love those who emigrated to them and find not any want in their breasts of what the emigrants were given but give [them] preference over themselves, even though they are in privation. And whoever is protected from the stinginess of his soul - it is those who will be the successful." (Surah Al-Hashr: Verse 9)

Allah said they didn't have ill feelings for what the migrants and refugees were given. They even give the refugee preferences over themselves even though they are in dire need. They prefer them (the migrants) and Allah S.W.T said "What is the secret?" Those who are saved from their own stinginess, they are the successful. Those who are saved from their own souls of greed and stinginess, they are those who are successful. This is the secret of the Ansar.

Chapter 5

Lessons from the Ansar

Prophet S.A.W when he was digging the trench with the *sahabahs* during the battle of the trench, the Ansar were digging and they were singing poetry. Then Prophet S.A.W was responding to them "Oh Allah, there is no life except for the life of the hereafter, so forgive the Muhajireen and the Ansar because of their love and the honesty that they had." Remember how the Ansar were toward the days of the end of Prophet S.A.W, they mentioned the gathering of Prophet S.A.W that they would miss? This is one of them.

The Prophet S.A.W after the battle of Hunain when he was giving out the war spoils, he distributed the war spoils among those who recently accepted Islam from the Muhajireen. However, he did not give anything to the Ansar. The Ansar were a little bit upset and questioned why they didn't get anything. They were sad because they thought the Prophet S.A.W preferred the people of Makkah over the people of Madinah.

Prophet S.A.W heard and gathered them and said "Oh Ansar, didn't I find you astray and Allah guided you the right way through me? And you were divided in groups and Allah brought you together through me?

And you were poor and Allah made you rich through me?" Every time they heard this from Prophet S.A.W, they started to feel bad. And they all said "Know that Allah and His Messenger is in favour of our blessings and we have even more than that. We're worse than what you said." The Ansar said "Allah deserves more, the Prophet S.A.W deserves more."

Look at Prophet Muhammad S.A.W's fairness where he then said "What prevents you from answering me?" The Ansar then asked "How should we respond to you?" Prophet S.A.W said "Say and be truthful when you say it, 'we're the ones (The Ansar) that gave you home and food, the ones who gave you refuge, the one welcomed you to Madinah', say that!" and the Ansar were quiet. He said "O Ansar, won't you be happy and pleased? People are going home with camels and sheep, golds and coins; and you're going to go home with the Prophet S.A.W to your homes."

"An Ansar is the inner cloth (garment) that we wear that touches the skin" was mentioned by Prophet Muhammad S.A.W. That's how close the Ansar are to the Prophet S.A.W. Other people are the jacket. When the Prophet said this, all of the Ansar started to cry and they said "We are happy and pleased as having Prophet S.A.W, as our portion in the share." What is the lesson from this? The Ansar did not take anything from this world, the only thing that they took from this world is the love of Prophet S.A.W.

Have a look on the *Khulafa Ar-Rasyidin*; who were kings, governors? We would not see the Ansar, we see the Muhajireen like Abu Hurairah, Saad ibn Waqqash, Khalid ibn Waleed, Umar Ibn Khattab, Abu Bakr, Abdullah ibn Masood; all of them were the Muhajireen. Where are the Ansar? The Ansar did not take anything from this world except the love of Prophet S.A.W. Meaning their hearts were too engrossed with wanting companionship with the Prophet S.A.W to be fighting over the leadership in this world. They didn't care because the Prophet S.A.W taught them that the best of the leaders are the best of followers.

That's what the Ansar knew. They said "Prophet S.A.W is our share and the portion of this *duniya*." So what else of this *duniya* is left for the Ansar? What wealth or material do they need after they had Prophet S.A.W? Reflect on ourselves when someone takes our position. We get upset and may start cursing and have this thing in our heart. Is this how a Muslim supposed to behave over leadership, position and material in this world? This is not what the Ansar were about.

Chapter 6

The Choices
in Life

The Prophet S.A.W continued the *khutbah* and said "O people, a servant from the servants of Allah has been given the decision between what is in this world and what is with Allah. His lord gave him a choice to live in this world however long he wishes and consume of this world however much he wishes; or that he meet his lord. So he chose meeting in his lord." Anas ibn Malik said "We heard Abu Bakr R.A burst out into tears and started to cry."

Where was Abu Bakr sitting? He was sitting at the back of the masjid. As Prophet S.A.W was telling the speech. Everyone was amazed at why was Abu Bakr crying and looking at the Prophet S.A.W. at front. Abu Bakr then said "Ya *Rasulullah*, we would sacrifice ourselves, ransom our children, mothers, fathers and wealth if we had to for you." The reason that we are amazed at Abu Bakr's crying was that he knew when Prophet S.A.W said "a servant was chosen", Prophet S.A.W himself was the servant he was referring to. Prophet Muhammad S.A.W was the one given the choice to remain in this world and consume the world as much as he wants or now to meet Allah S.A.W. Abu Bakr realised that because he was the most knowledgeable one and knew what Prophet S.A.W even meant.

Prophet Muhammad S.A.W does not want us to be people who are engrossed into this world and making our lives into about what is our next car to buy. What business transaction to do to make more money. To be too engrossed in it, not just live and make a means for my family. We live in the world that is filled with bustling gains of wealth. When the call of *Zuhr* comes, we see some who would take breaks from their work to go to their masjid and perform *Zuhr*. While some are so engrossed in their worldly material that the hereafter can be postpone to later.

The Prophet S.A.W is teaching us, don't be engrossed. In fact, when we're so engrossed with this world it's called *Ittiba al Hawa*; following this desire for wealth, gaining and status. When we follow our desire, it will make us fall into a black hole of emptiness. Feeling empty and depressed. We will feel like there is no purpose. We have everything in our life, the best clothes, the best house and everything. But why do we feel empty? Because we have engrossed ourselves with something that is temporary. It will not give us fulfillment.

In fact, if we are so self-engrossed with this, Imam Al-Ghazali said it will lead us to feeling dissatisfied with the *Qadr* of Allah. It is as if we're angry at why Allah gave us only this limited amount. This dissatisfaction is what leading many people with depression. Many people feel sadness, where some people do have medical depression but that is a separate discussion that requires medical attention and counsellors. We're talking about societal engrossment for more and feeling displeased with what Allah gave them. They are not content with their spouse, wealth and job. Their discontentment is not a motivation to do more, but discontentment of what Allah gave them in the first place.

The Prophet S.A.W reminded us with one of the most powerful reminders of the *khutbah* that we were given the choice of consume and stay content as much as we want and this is what we are here for in this world; or we can choose the meeting of our Lord. This is what Abu Bakr R.A realised. Prophet S.A.W heard Abu Bakr crying at the back of the masjid and he knew why Abu Bakr was crying. It's because only Abu Bakr understood the final words of *Rasulullah* S.A.W. The Prophet S.A.W then said "Calm down Abu Bakr, don't cause a panic among the people".

The One to
Love Dearly

Allah S.W.T then continued to teach us a lesson with our Prophet S.A.W. Prophet S.A.W then said "If I were to take a *khaleel* (a close dear companion), I would have taken Abu Bakr as my *khaleel*. But there is not *khaleel* except for Allah S.W.T". What does this mean? *Khaleel* means the most love that we can have in our heart for something. Some people's *khaleel* is their car, they would kill if someone did anything to their car. Some people's *khaleel* is their job, spouse, girlfriend or boyfriend. They will do anything for this creation. Nonetheless, the Prophet S.A.W taught us a lesson. The only *khaleel* for a humanbeing can be is Allah S.W.T. What is a *khaleel*?

Do we know who the *khaleel* of Allah S.W.T is? Prophet Ibrahim A.S. Why was he called *al-khaleel*? What was the greatest test in Ibrahim's life? To sacrifice his son. If we think rationally, why would Allah need him to sacrifice his son? An easy answer would be because Allah The All-Knowing knew he would not have to sacrifice his son, but Allah wanted to give us a lesson. What is the most beloved thing to a human being? Their children right? We would do anything to for our children.

Allah S.W.T wanted to teach humanity that even through a child, Ibrahim A.S was tested with so that he could leave nothing in his heart, except for Allah. That because of the love of Allah, he loved the child. Allah S.W.T and His wisdom will never ask us to harm our child, so it was symbolic. By the time Prophet Ibrahim wanted to sacrifice, Allah S.W.T said "Stop, you passed the test. You left nothing in your heart, except for *khullah* – except that Allah is your *khaleel*". Allah declared Prophet Ibrahim is the closest companion of Allah S.W.T.

Our Prophet Muhammad S.A.W said "I was blessed with this in the final five days of my life. Allah has blessed me now that I am his *khaleel*"; just like how Prophet Ibrahim was Allah's *khaleel*. Now there is no place in Prophet Muhammad S.A.W's heart except Allah S.W.T. If there were to be a place, who would that be? Aisha? Umar? Ali R.A? He said Abu Bakr. Meaning the closest creation, in love, reverence and respect is Abu Bakr to Prophet S.A.W. Think about how much love that is.

Think about us, when we think about the person we're in love with, while staring at the sky. For some people it might be the opposite gender, a future husband or wife if Allah wills. Abu Bakr was so beloved to the Prophet S.A.W, he used to think about Abu Bakr and asked where he would be. Prophet S.A.W used to tell stories to Aisha with excitement and would tell his stories with Abu Bakr always being included in it; out of his love and companionship to Abu Bakr. This is what Prophet S.A.W wanted us to learn, to have Allah as our *khaleel* more than how we love another person dearly.

Imam Ghazali said "The *khaleel* is the one who presses every aspect of his heart openly and inwardly only for Allah S.W.T" this is the *khaleel* for Allah. This is what we're all trying to reach and overcome on a day to day issue. If we were given one million right now, what would we do? We would be jumping up and down and praise Allah. Cause we would be so excited. What is the *khaleel*? The *khaleel* is the heart with Allah and constantly ask "How is this pleasing Allah? Where did this money come from?" Every movement is for Allah S.W.T, our *salam* to our brothers or sisters is because we think of Allah. Prophet S.A.W said "Even when putting the food into the mouth of our child or wife is for Allah S.W.T"

Imam Ghazali also said something beautiful, he said "*Ikhlas* has three levels, the level of a slave, the level of a merchant and the level of a lover." What is *ikhlas* at the level of a slave? It is when we do something because fear of Allah's punishment. For example, when we do charity, it is to extinguish the anger of Allah and it is solely for Allah and His forgiveness. This is the lowest level of *ikhlas* or sincerity.

The second level of sincerity at the level of a merchant. It is that we intend when we are doing something to get reward from Allah. We intend it with a benefit from Allah S.W.T has given us in that action. For example, whoever fasts one day Allah S.W.T will make them distant 70 years from the hellfire. We fast and we want this reward, or for certain level of *Jannah*. Another example is praying 12 of their sunnah every single day, Allah S.W.T builds a castle for them in *Jannah* or gives up an argument, even though they are the right one and say it's not worth it, Allah will place them the best part of *Jannah*.

The highest and the best level of *ikhlas* is the sincerity at the level of a lover. It is when we are doing something solely because of the love for Allah. The intention of doing a good deed with the action of doing it out of the pure pleasure of Allah. Allah loves this, so we want to do this. All of the levels of *ikhlas* are fine, but this is the highest level. This is *khullah*, the dearest love to the One and Only, Allah; this is *khaleel*.

Chapter 8

The Timeless Legacy

This contents of the final sermon by Prophet S.A.W was a set of reminder for us to live with. When he said this, he gave a command to his ummah which is legacy. The first of which, was for the community; the Ansar. He wanted his ummah to be the Ansar. The second of which is for Allah S.W.T and the third of which is his legacy that he left behind and that everyone is to close their door of the *masajid*, except for the door of Abu Bakr.

Why? Let the one who was in the companionship of the Prophet S.A.W, who was disciplined by the Prophet, who was taught by the Prophet, who was the closest to the Prophet, who emulated the Prophet S.A.W, who knew what the Prophet thought, and who knew even what Prophet Muhammad S.A.W meant to say. Let him lead this ummah. This is a legacy of Prophet S.A.W. Who is to lead the legacy of this ummah? The one whom emulated Prophet S.A.W not just outwardly, but the one who empathise like the Prophet empathises and the one who thinks of humanity like our Prophet S.A.W.

This is the doorway of our master, Abu Bakr As-Siddiq. As if *Rasulullah* S.A.W said leadership and the legacy of this ummah are only those who follow the footsteps of Abu Bakr. So close our doors to leaderships, there is no door other than Abu Bakr. There is no door to power or to lead this ummah with righteousness, except those who lived like Abu Bakr. This was the legacy of *Rasulullah* S.A.W. Understand the power of this message. Look at the things our Prophet S.A.W talked about in this beautiful farewell *khutbah*, in few short words, he got the message across to the ummah to this day.

Prophet *alaihi salatu wa salam* stepped down from the mimbar and the *sahabahs* knew they would never get to see Prophet S.A.W again. The last time they saw *Rasulullah* S.A.W, his one final time was when the Prophet S.A.W at his house and the *sahabahs* were in a *solah* in Masjid An-Nabawi. The *solah* was being led by Abu Bakr R.A. The Prophet S.A.W opened the curtains, he looked at his ummah being led by the one thing that will give us all the sanity in this world, *solah*. By the one who will carry on his legacy, Abu Bakr R.A and the Prophet S.A.W smiled, his beautiful smile.

Anas R.A said because Prophet S.A.W did that, they almost wanted to leave their *soluh* and go to the

Prophet S.A.W out of their love and happiness that they saw him, but the Prophet S.A.W motioned with his hand for them to stay. The curtains then fell and that was the last time they saw the Prophet S.A.W, the beautiful smile of Prophet S.A.W. This is the final *khutbah* of Prophet S.A.W. When he left this earth, his last words in this world was "Oh Allah, the highest companionship".

Make a promise to ourselves. What does it take for us to be like the Ansar? The Prophet S.A.W said to the Ansar, "After me, you will see others given preference to you; but have patience until you meet me. I will meet you at the head of the *hawd* (it is a pool made from the Fountain of Al-Kauthar in paradise, flooded and made into a pool in Madinah at the mimbar of Prophet Muhammad S.A.W)" (Sahih Bukhari) and all of the Ansar will be gathered there and then the rest of the believers. And the people of Madinah will be the first resurrected to the Prophet S.A.W.

Prophet S.A.W said "You go through difficulty, you go through hardship, someone speaking evil about you, they're taking visions of leadership, taking the lives of your fellow brother and sisters, they're committing injustice, oppression and racism; have patience. Try your best and you will meet me at this location." We will meet in Madinah at the home of Prophet Muhammad S.A.W. Anas R.A. said the Prophet S.A.W said when he looked at the Ansar, "I swear by Allah, you are the most beloved people to me; the Ansar."

Why? They love nothing on this earth, except for the love of *Rasulullah* S.A.W. They never vide for this world just like their Prophet never vide for it and they were genuine people who tried to help no matter who was in front of them. Imagine that Allah gives us this opportunity. Allah tests us every day by placing someone that is need of something from us, to see what we will do. Try it, it may be even going to the masjid and we see an old uncle or aunty on the road.

We have two options, we drive to the masjid then go to work. Or we stop the car and help this old aunty or uncle go where they need to go. And who is watching? Only Allah S.W.T. Maybe someone comes up to us and said "I need something to eat, I'm hungry" and we go buy some food. Or even we get the opportunity to go to Syria, Kashmir, Yemen or wherever and we are there to help them. Think, what is our test today that we would be like the Ansar and what love of the Prophet S.A.W that we need to have in our hearts.

Have the desire that we need to learn more about Prophet Muhammad S.A.W. We ask Allah for us to be like our Prophet S.A.W and those that are close to him. To give us the love of the Ansar and the love of those who are blessed by Allah. We ask Allah S.W.T to allow us to visit the city of Madinah for those who have not and who have. We ask Allah S.W.T to have us buried in the city with Prophet Muhammad S.A.W with his Ansar, Abu Bakr, Umar, Uthman and all of the *sahabahs* and to gather with Ali R.A in the highest level of *Jannah*. May Allah bless all of us, make us those who are genuine-like as Prophet S.A.W. spoke of.

Discussions (Q&A)

QUESTION:

We see that people who are in need asking for money almost every day and we may start thinking, isn't this person fully able to work (rather than asking for money)?

ANSWER:

We need to look at the locality and the society. If our community provide support for people of such situation, then one of the way is to provide and show them where they can get help. Some people may require us to ask them personally of their situation. For example, some societies make it impossible for women to work, this may require us to give the only instead. *Wallahu ʿalam.*

QUESTION:

What is the ruling on giving to the non-muslims?

ANSWER:

Yes, we can give funds to the non-muslims. Even Prophet S.A.W supported his Jewish neighbour. There is a category in charity even to give to the non-muslims so their hearts can become closer to Islam; even if they are in need or not in need. It is not bribery; it is a genuine act that we do not care about the money but when we treat the non-muslims for a meal or such, is as a form of sadaqah (charity) and it is acceptable.

There are certain situations where we give money and they may spend it on drugs or something that is not good, but if giving money as a form of charity makes us questionable, give in the form of item instead such as food, clothing or offer help such as informing them about the shelter locations or job opportunities nearby. As far as helping anyone regardless of religion, this is part of humanity and this is what our faith teaches us to do.

QUESTION:

A friend of mine gives money with the intention just to help people and not even putting a clear intention from it; just to help. Anybody who is in need of help, he gives money. Is this deed rewarded?

ANSWER:

Yes, it is rewarded since the reward for helping somebody is intended. But the reward of helping people with the intention for Allah, the reward is higher. The idea is, we must have the mental awareness that helping another person is for Allah because Allah loves those who do it for Him. There is always reward, but remember the levels of *ikhlas*, before we do a good deed, take a second and say, this is for Allah. This is why *ikhlas* and *niat* are challenging. Make it a habit, take a moment to set our intention for Allah.

QUESTION:

How do we stop ourselves from being overly proud of ourselves, especially after doing a good deed?

ANSWER:

Having pride that is out of our control, will lead us towards *shaitaan*. It will make us do things out of rational and out of intellect. The best of believers is the one who is Allah-conscious, self-sufficient, light-hearted and do not hold grudges to other people. Arrogance and haste will make us commit the mistakes that our father Adam A.S made. How to control it? Purify our souls, knowledge and put it into practice, such as being patient and not being arrogant on our souls.

QUESTION:

How do we know when we have given enough?

ANSWER:

It is unlikely that we know when we have given enough to others. Why? Because Allah S.W.T is worth more than anything. For example of the *dua'a* by Prophet Yunus A.S. that we may practice to this day "There is no deity except You; exalted are You. Indeed, I have been of the wrongdoers." (Surah Al-Anbiya: Verse 87). Why do we make this *dua'a*? Because no matter how much *solah* and dhikr we make, it's never enough for us to say we have done enough for Allah S.W.T. So do our best and hardest, then leave it to Al-Kareem, Allah - The Generous. Nonetheless, Allah does reminds us when we do want to help people, don't forget ourselves; get good education, stable job with great income to help others.

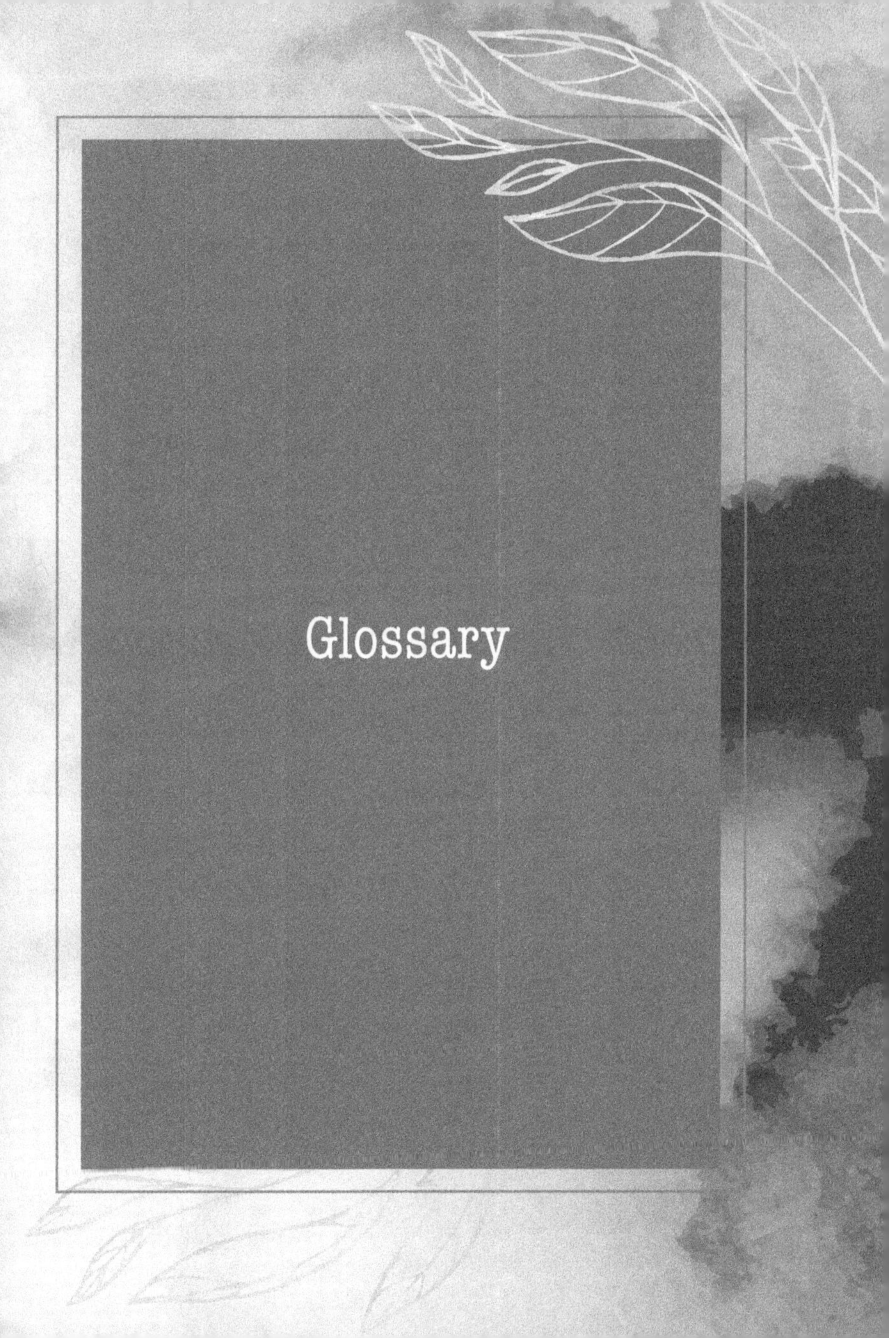

Glossary

Alaihi salatu wa salam	On Him (Muhammad) are the blessings and the peace of Allah
Allahumma salli ala sayyidina	O Allah! Send Your Blessings upon our Master Muhammad
Dhikr	Reminding oneself; a short ritual prayer for the purpose of glorifying and remembrance of Allah
Dua'a	Supplication
Duniya	Temporal world and its earthly concerns and possessions
Habib	Beloved
Ikhlas	Sincerity
Istighfar	A short prayer of redemption; in the literal sense, "I seek forgiveness from Allah"
Jannah	Garden; in Islam is referred to as Paradise
Khaleel	intimate friend, close companion

Khulafa Ar-Rasyidin	The Four Caliphs were the first four leaders of Islam that succeeded the Prophet Muhammad. Abu Bakr As-Siddiq, Umar Ibn Khattab, Uthman Ibn Affan and Ali Ibn Abi Talib; The Rashidun Caliphate.
Khutbah	Sermon
Mimbar	The pulpit where sermons were given; where Prophet Muhammad gave his sermon
Muamalah	Transactions or dealings
Nabi	Prophet
Niat	Intention
Qadr	Decree or fate
Radiallahu anha/ anhu (R.A.)	May Allah be pleased with her/ him
Rakaat	A single unit of Islamic prayer (solah)
Rasulullah	Messenger

S.A.W	Sallahualaihi Wa Salam - peace be upon him (Prophet Muhammad S.A.W)
S.W.T	Subhanahu Wa Ta'ala - Glory to Him - Allah, the Exalted
Sahabahs	Companions; Friends and family who lived in the times of Prophet Muhammad S.A.W.
Shaitaan	The devil; evil spirit
Solah	Prayer; a form of worship that is obligated five times a day for a Muslim
Sunnah	Tradition or way; in Islam is referred as any words and actions by the Prophet S.A.W
Ummah	The whole community of Muslims bound together by ties of religion
Zuhr	The midday Islamic prayer, when the sun reaches its zenith; one of the five obligatory prayers in Islam

Epilogue

Khutbatul Wada' – The last and farewell sermon of our beloved Prophet Muhammad S.A.W (Peace be upon him). The sermon that contained the very last few reminders from the Prophet S.A.W before his passing. It is stated that his passing is the greatest calamity the ummah has to face.

However, the love of Prophet Muhammad S.A.W towards his ummah was extremely profound that during his last few days of life and during the very last time of stepping on the *mimbar* (pulpit of sermon), he conveyed consequential reminders that are significant from the times of the Muslims among the companions and the Ansar until to the Muslims of this day.

The reminders that are timeless which are to be accompanied with the Qur'an and Sunnah to prepare individuals to endure the challenges and difficulties in life without the Prophet Muhammad S.A.W. A man who was sent by Allah S.W.T to be followed and guidance of faith to paradise; peace and blessings upon him every day, Prophet Muhammad.

Notes

Notes

NEW BOOKS

BY HASIB NOOR

FAREWELL
THE LAST SERMON OF OUR BELOVED

QUOTES BOOK
PRACTICAL SPIRITUALITY

SHOP ONLINE

WWW.TERTIB.PRESS

REACH
THE SWEETNESS
OF PRAYER
MOUTASEM AL-HAWEEDY

THE BENEFICIAL MEANS TO
A HAPPY LIFE
MOUTASEM AL-HAWEEDY

The Path Seekers
ALAA ELSAYED

A JUZ A DAY
SUMMARY OF THE QUR'AN
YAHYA IBRAHIM

LOVE STORIES from the QUR'AN
YAHYA IBRAHIM

TEARFUL MOMENTS OF RASULULLAH
YAHYA IBRAHIM

I LOST MY WAY
FINDING HAPPINESS AFTER DESPAIR
YASMIN MOGAHED

Shattered Glass
Healing A Broken Heart
Yasmin Mogahed

The Miracle of the Qur'an
DR. YASIR QADHI

ALLAH LOVES ...
OMAR SULEIMAN

REPENTANCE
Omar Suleiman

THE POWER OF REPENTANCE
DR. YASIR QADHI